# THE Christ
## OF CHRISTMAS

# THE Christ
## OF CHRISTMAS

*Readings for Advent*

31 DAYS OF DEVOTIONS BY
## Calvin Miller
*Featuring the Holman Christian Standard Bible®*

## DEDICATION

*To my good friend, Lawrence Kimbrough,
who often makes my writing sound better than it is.*

# INTRODUCTION

Much of Christmas' beauty is in its sameness. The same traditions. The same meals. The same songs. The same story. Yet each Christmas is a little different. Sometimes the change is noticeable and unexpected, at other times a mere matter of flexibility. But each year's celebration somehow speaks its familiar message with a freshness that can only be heard by ears a year older.

So you're invited to bring your this-Christmas life within reach of God's Christmas story, to look at these same pictures of love and grace from a new vantage point, to spend a few moments each day letting God's comforting sameness reveal His new-every-morning side.

You can use these devotional readings by yourself or with your whole family. If you have a little more time and want to make the experience even more significant, an additional Scripture passage has been included for you to look up each day, along with some related thoughts and questions to consider.

You'll also notice that the readings continue through the end of December. The days following Christmas are important ones, where the lessons of Jesus' birth can find a natural link with the new year.

May this gentle journey through the Advent season draw you ever closer to the Christ of Christmas.

# DECEMBER 1

*There was a man named John who was sent from God. He came as a witness to testify about the light, so that all might believe through him. He was not the light, but he came to testify about the light.* JOHN 1:6-9

# ONLY A MAN NAMED JOHN

His name was John. He was born to be the forerunner of Christ, born to bear witness of the light.

In a way, John was like us. We, too, have been born to bear witness of that light. Each time we approach the Advent season, we become joyously occupied with celebrating what the light has done in our lives. While John the Baptist was the first person called to be a witness of that light, His calling has become ours.

John knew people would always be critical of the light. The light has always had to shine in a darkness that fails to appreciate it. Still, though the darkness rejects it, the light of witness shines still.

What does it mean to be a witness of the light? It simply means that we point to Jesus and say, *See, Jesus is the light of the world!* How did John the Baptist do this? Well, when he first saw Jesus coming to the Jordan River, he pointed to Him and cried,

TO STAND IN AN UNCARING WORLD AND SAY, "SEE, HERE IS THE CHRIST" IS A DARING ACT OF COURAGE.

"Here is the Lamb of God, who takes away the sin of the world! This is the One I told you about." John's job was not to coerce those around him to accept his announcement as truth. Nor did Jesus expect him to make believers all by himself. Like John, we cannot make believers. Believers make themselves by voluntarily coming to faith, one at a time.

But like John, we can point to Christ and say with all of our hearts, "Here is the Lamb of God!"

What if they do not believe us? No matter. We have done our best to tell them of God's grace. God will never hold us accountable for being ineffective in pointing the way. But He will hold us accountable for our cowardly silences. Being an effective witness means that we call attention to our testimony and leave the results to Him. Anything else—anything less—is failing the expectations of God.

We are born again; we must bear witness!

# AN ADDITIONAL READING

*Read: Acts 1:6-11*

Christmas is a door thrown open, a season like few others. *Christ* is the first part of the word *Christmas*—a syllable of joy on everyone's tongue. Are your eyes open wide? Is your heart alive with the hope of pointing someone to a gift like none other? Promise you'll be watching, listening, sharing. This Christmas, keep your light turned on.

# PRAYER

*Lord,* I want people around me to know that I believe You are the light of the world. I want to love You so much that people can see in my life—even if they never listen to my words—that I believe You are the light of the world. I know that making my witness visible, in and of itself, is not enough. I must have courage in the presence of my friends to point to You and say clearly, "Behold, the Lamb of God! Behold, the light of the world." If I continue to walk silently while others are walking in darkness, it is my own fault, for You, Jesus, are the light of my life—of all life.

# DECEMBER 2

*The Word became flesh and took up residence among us. We observed His glory, the glory as the unique Son from the Father, full of grace and truth.*                JOHN 1:14

# THE GLORY WE BEHELD

The glory we behold in Christ is the light of grace and truth. Consider this great trinity of words: glory, grace, and truth.

*Glory!* It is the state of being that transcends our poor, dull, ordinary lives. It implies a dazzling illumination, a splendor in seeing, a heightened euphoria, a state of elevated reality. Glory is that moment of elation when truth and reward come together to kneel before the grand approval of God. Have you never felt His exhilarating glory? Then you have never confessed your sin and turned your face toward the wonderful face of your Redeemer. Glory is the glistening garment of God—a garment that He is all too eager to throw around us, to welcome us into His everlasting light. Glory is the food of the believer. Eat it once, and a kind of joyous addiction is born in your life. One taste and you must eat it forever.

*Grace!* It is the unmerited smile of God. If glory is our dance with God, grace is the ballroom—wide and free. But grace is not a tiny little dance with thin music and stingy steps. This dance never constricts. It is set to the open steps of elation. Grace saves with celestial music and redeems us, with Christ as our life partner.

*Truth!* This is the mortar that binds grace and glory together. Truth is Jesus; He never told a lie. He never sinned. He is never out of love with those for whom He died. Truth says that when you take any action, needing God to be there, He will be there. Truth says that if Jesus has said it, it is settled; you may count on it.

Jesus was revealed to us in glory. That glory is full of grace and truth. The moment you received Christ, all three—glory, grace, and truth—were united as a trinity of lovers to rule from the throne of all your dreams.

GLORY, GRACE, AND TRUTH. RECEIVE THEM FREELY, FOR THEY CAN NEVER BE BOUGHT.

# AN ADDITIONAL READING

*Read: First Thessalonians 4:13-18*

We have grown so accustomed to this particular coming of Christ—this baby-in-a-manger coming, this wise-men-and-shepherds coming—that we sometimes forget to be watching for His next coming. What keeps His next coming from being a more real part of your life? What is here now that won't be so much better then?

# PRAYER

*Lord,* I have beheld Your glory, full of grace and truth. What a life is now mine—glory, grace, and truth bulging in the same small space I once gave to dullness, stinginess, and deceit. And what a life now awaits me—glory, grace, and truth in greater measure than I have ever imagined. I love You for filling my heart with Your presence, for being just what my dull heart needed.

# DECEMBER 3

*Salmon fathered Boaz by Rahab, Boaz fathered Obed by Ruth, Obed fathered Jesse, and Jesse fathered King David . . . . and Jacob fathered Joseph the husband of Mary, who gave birth to Jesus who is called Messiah.*

MATTHEW 1:5-6 AND 1:16

# ONE MAN'S FAMILY

In older versions of the Bible, these genealogies are called the *begat* passages. This idea of *begetting* means to sire a child, to conceive a newborn baby. It is a genetic word, as we modern people might see it. But God uses these *begat* words as a calling to His lost family.

So the begat passages seem dull to you? Read them again and think of how God elevated the idea of family by choosing to work with one man's family to redeem the earth. These begat passages are not just names. They are the footprints of a timeless God walking through the generations, until His tread is reduced to the bare foot of the little baby Mary held in her arms.

All international and civil struggles could be cleared up if we could agree on this one-man's-family view of the human race. God has always held this view. He created Adam and Eve, and from them came the human family. But God's bright hopes for His family were spoiled. Adam and Eve lost Eden. Their quarreling children Cain and Abel marked the earth with ruin. Their grandchildren fostered quarreling nations who brought death and dying to a never-ending reign of bloodshed.

But God never gave up His plan that this one family united in love and eternal life would redeem the world. So in time the genealogies would spiral down from generation to generation until at last came the family of Jesse, from whose lineage came a line of kings. Then one day Mary held an infant in her arms. From this child would come the completed dream of God:

> ONCE GRACE HAS SCRUBBED THE SOUL, ANYONE CAN TAKE THEIR PLACE IN THE LINEAGE OF THE SON OF GOD.

"When the completion of the time came, God sent His son, born of a woman, born under the law, to redeem those under the law, so that we might receive adoption as sons. And because you are sons, God has sent the Spirit of His Son into our hearts, crying '*Abba*, Father!' So you are no longer a slave, but a son; and if a son, then an heir through God" (Galatians 4:4-7).

So the begat passages remind us that God is the Father of all who will call Jesus Lord. Once we call Him Lord, we begin to love the God who sent His Son as the final name in a long line of begats. In Him is our hope. He is God's finally begotten Son, God's only begotten Son. Because of Him, we call God "*Abba*, Father."

# AN ADDITIONAL READING

*Read: John 14:23-26*

Jesus' words to His followers sound for all the world like a family in conversation. His words are reminders of how much He loves them. They exist as instructions on what to do in certain situations, news about a friend who's coming to live close by. Our homes and families can sometimes be sources of struggle. But His reality is for every family a source of constant care. Doesn't that feel good at Christmas?

## PRAYER

*Lord,* the family of God is my family now. How odd they sometimes look: different colors, different languages, different customs and values. Thank You so much for making me a part of Your worldwide dream of calling Your entire human family back to the adoration of Your only begotten Son.

# DECEMBER 4

$T$he angel said to him: "Do not be afraid, Zachariah, because your prayer has been heard. Your wife Elizabeth will bear you a son, and you will name him John."

LUKE 1:13

# WHEN OLD MEN TRUST

Trust is sometimes hard to hold on to. It is like its dear sister, Hope. Trust blatantly affirms: *I believe, even though I have not the tiniest shred of evidence to demonstrate it. What do I believe? I believe God is yet on His throne and that all He has promised me, He will do. If you want to see broken confidence, you need not examine me, for my trust will forever stand. It is as unstoppable as Niagara, for it clings to the God who created Niagara.*

> IT IS A SIN TO QUIT BELIEVING TOO EARLY, BEFORE WE HAVE FOUND OUR USEFULNESS TO GOD.

Zachariah was an old man. All his life he had served in the temple, giving God all he had. Is there not something wonderful about old men and women who have loved God all their lives? Even in their old age they cannot quit dreaming. Whatever life is left to them will surely unfold some greater deed that they may do for God.

Zachariah received the answer to his yearning. He would have a son and name him John. With such a promise came a child of significance. God had special things in mind for this child, and that special purpose gave an old man a heart-gladness whose music could not be silenced.

When old men trust, they become the life partners of God. When are we ever through trusting? We never are, and the older our trust the greater our confidence.

Juxtapose this old man and his little son—a leathery face against a newborn baby's skin. A child and the purpose of God held in wrinkled old hands. Best of all was the certain knowledge that God honors trust.

Have you wanted something from God? Are you weary of asking Him? Have you wearied in your hope, thinking surely God has forgotten you? Remember Zachariah.

Do not despair.
Trust is always
rewarded.

## AN ADDITIONAL READING

*Read: Luke 2:25-38*

Jesus' birth, too, was greeted by aging eyes—those whose wrinkles betrayed a faith still young and vibrant—trust that never had much use for getting old and cynical. Has your faith in God's promises grown old before your years? How refreshing to realize that a believing heart keeps the shoulders straight and the body alert.

## PRAYER

*Lord,* I need Zachariah's example. I so often complain that my faith goes unrewarded. I would like to learn the art of walking by faith, even when it seems Your promises are delayed. Make trust the appetizer to every feast of Your abundance. Make trust my meal, and for the dessert I'll have another helping of the same.

# DECEMBER 5

*H*e came to her and said, "Rejoice, favored woman! The Lord is with you." But she was deeply troubled by this statement and was wondering what kind of greeting this could be. Then the angel told her: "Do not be afraid, Mary, for you have found favor with God."                    LUKE 1:28-30

# OUT OF THE ORDINARY

God's visitations unnerve us. Why? Because He never comes to us without asking us to do something. We never know what He will ask of us, but we know that we will be overwhelmed by our feelings of inadequacy. When God came to Moses, Moses said, *Ask Aaron!* When He came to Gideon, Gideon suggested, *Let's put out the fleece, God.* When God asks us for anything, we are prone to say, *God, even though this is a great honor, would You mind honoring someone else?* So God came to Mary of Nazareth. As is always the case, God was the very last person she was expecting.

• *"Rejoice, favored woman! The Lord is with you."* God generally promises us His steadfast presence before He asks of us some task we feel is beyond us.

• *"Do not be afraid!"* God often says this—just before He terrifies us with His demand. For although He calls us to do something significant, we generally feel we cannot do it.

- *"Mary, you have found favor with God!"* This promise of grace is a statement of special notice. Mary, above all the women of Nazareth, had been singled out by God. Did she not find God's special notice a little disturbing? Of course! Every time God says, *I want you!*—(as He did to Mary)—our next question is, *Why are You talking to me? There must be fifteen million people who can do this job better than I can.*

There is no answer to this issue of grace. *You are the chosen one, Mary,* replied God. *This is all! Discussion over!*

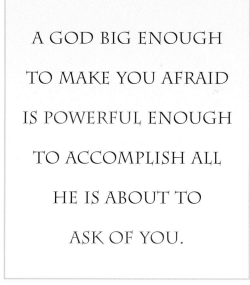

A GOD BIG ENOUGH

TO MAKE YOU AFRAID

IS POWERFUL ENOUGH

TO ACCOMPLISH ALL

HE IS ABOUT TO

ASK OF YOU.

# AN ADDITIONAL READING

*Read: Luke 2:25-38*

*Jesus, don't come in yet! The floor's not done! Your room's not ready!* We modern-day Marthas are sure that Jesus wouldn't want to stay with us until we'd vacuumed and dusted. How much we need to be like her sister Mary, who simply left her dirty dishes on the table. After all, Jesus would know best how to put them away.

# PRAYER

*Lord,* may I quit trying to figure out the mathematics of grace. You have chosen me because it is Your nature to use the bewildered. And that is enough for me. What would You have me to do?

# DECEMBER 6

*"Now listen: You will conceive and give birth to a son, and you will call His name JESUS. He will be great and will be called the Son of the Most High, and the Lord God will give Him the throne of His father David. He will reign over the house of Jacob forever, and His kingdom will have no end."*

LUKE 1:31-33

# CALL HIM THE DELIVERER

Once Mary was past the stupefaction of giving birth to the Son of God, three things became apparent to her. First, she was to be given an assignment. Second, she was to be given information on what to do with the assignment. Third, she was told what the assignment meant.

• Gabriel's first word: *"You will conceive and give birth to a Son."* Notice how the assignment came first. This assignment must have been staggering to a young, unmarried woman. But before she could protest the assignment, she was given the information she would need to accomplish it.

• Gabriel's second word: *"You will call His name JESUS!"* She received all the information necessary to execute the will of God. God is like that. He never offers us an assignment without giving us all the information we need to accomplish it.

- Gabriel's third word: *"He will be great and will be called the Son of the Most High, and the Lord God will give Him the throne of His father David. He will reign over the house of Jacob forever, and His kingdom will have no end."*

Consider what the assignment and the accompanying information meant. All of this procedural revelation given at the annunciation of Jesus' birth did not make the news easy to deal with, but it does say that God did not choose Mary to do something and then leave her in the dark to deal with it. God's love for those whom He chooses always understands the heaviness that comes with His requirements. It always reaches to embrace those who have had to learn to agree to the word *Lord* out of great fear and trembling.

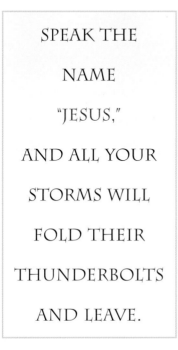

SPEAK THE NAME "JESUS," AND ALL YOUR STORMS WILL FOLD THEIR THUNDERBOLTS AND LEAVE.

## AN ADDITIONAL READING

*Read: Isaiah 43:1-3a*

You are covered under God's insurance plan. To be sure, He places a premium on getting His work done, on making His name known, on claiming glory for His wondrous love and power. But He also makes sure that those who accomplish great things in His service are protected, cared for, equipped, and encouraged. There's no safer place to live than the center of His will.

## PRAYER

*Lord,* how thorough You are in Your loving instruction. How wonderful! People who thought they were too small to do Your will are delighted to find that You empower them for all You ask. When my frail obedience has run its course, I marvel that I am able to be of any use to You. I never saw myself as talented enough to serve You, but Your faithful presence has never left me. Thank You, Lord Jesus.

# DECEMBER 7

$\mathcal{M}$ary asked the angel, "How can this be, since I have not been intimate with a man?" The angel replied to her: "The Holy Spirit will come upon you, and the power of the Most High will overshadow you. Therefore the holy child to be born will be called the Son of God." LUKE 1:34-35

# WHEN GOD EXPLAINS HIMSELF

Have you ever hungered to understand the mysteries of God? So did Mary. *"How can this be?"* she asked. Even angels cannot explain the mysteries that underlie the miracles. We must learn to relax and trust the inscrutable God. For mystery is the heart of faith! Wrestle with it in the light, and it will evaporate. But enjoy the mysteries of God in all their hiddenness, and your life will thrive on the power of a God too vast for you to track.

How often we want to explain what we cannot figure out. But nothing that brings ultimate meaning to our lives is explainable. Such things are always beyond the safe, settled reach of the predictable. Consider this list of ultimate miracles, for they rest on the piers of an unsolvable mystery:

• *The new birth.* Jesus said this new birth was like the wind; we can hear the sound of it but cannot tell where it comes from or where it is going. "So it is with everyone born of the Spirit" (John 3:8). Salvation is both as mysterious and certain as the wind.

• *Our position in heaven.* When James and John asked Jesus for positions of power in the new kingdom, He said, "To sit at My right and left is not Mine to give; instead, it belongs to those for whom it has been prepared by My Father" (Matthew 20:23). Jesus had to say that our position in heaven must remain a mystery while we are here on earth.

- *The time of His second coming.* When asked when He would come to restore His kingdom on earth, Jesus said, "It is not for you to know times or periods that the Father has set by His own authority" (Acts 1:7). We are not allowed to know the time of His second coming, yet this mystery thrills us with moment-by-moment anticipation and expectancy.

Many people have experienced the mystery of things too wonderful and too gloriously real ever to be explained. Yet such mysteries envelop our redemption. Paul knew he could never explain God; he confessed that "the mystery of godliness is great" (1 Timothy 3:16). Mary at last came to understand that wonderful things happen when the Holy Spirit comes upon us and the power of the Almighty overshadows us.

MARY SUBMITTED HERSELF TO THE MYSTERY THAT GOD'S HOWS ARE NEVER VERY RATIONAL, BUT HIS REDEMPTION IS ETERNAL.

## AN ADDITIONAL READING

*Read: Romans 11:33-36*

We basically have two choices to make in dealing with the mysteries of God. We can wrestle with Him or we can rest in Him. We can continue searching the unsearchable or relax in the reality. What exists at the end of all our searching will be a God who knows absolutely everything . . . and chooses to love us anyway.

## PRAYER

*Lord,* it is a great comfort to know that I have a God too big to be explained by human logic. Yet in these great inscrutable mysteries I find the new birth, the second coming, and all things glorious.

# DECEMBER 8

*"Consider Elizabeth your relative—even she has conceived a son in her old age, and this is the sixth month for her who was called barren. For nothing will be impossible with God." "Consider me the Lord's slave," said Mary. "May it be done for me according to your word."* LUKE 1:36-37

# GLORIOUS IMPOSSIBILITIES

Why would anyone ever want a God of the possible? Consider His every act of significance in your life. How many of those acts have you ever been able to figure out?

• Is it possible that at one time you were dead in Christ with no destiny or hope, but now you are born again in a life that will outlast the stars? *Celebrate this glorious impossibility!*

• Is it possible that the name of Christ meant nothing to you at one time, and yet now you cannot conceive of living a single day without His presence? *Celebrate this glorious impossibility!*

• Is it possible that you once feared death, but now you know that Jesus Christ, this little baby of Bethlehem, has come out of the grave, renovating all your bogus pride and transforming your fears into hope? *Celebrate this glorious impossibility!*

We must look to Mary's example to know how to deal with the glorious impossibilities of God. Look how she turned the world upside down by making one simple statement: *"Consider me the Lord's slave. May it be done to me according to your word."* Can it be that one very young and insignificant woman changed the world just by agreeing to the mysteries of God? It can indeed! God needs only a little of our agreement in order to work mighty wonders.

When the most ordinary of people say, *"Consider me the Lord's slave,"* churches are born, hospitals rise, Christian universities come to be. Some of the greatest missionaries were born when a timid believer agreed, *"Consider me the Lord's slave."*

Perhaps even now you are hungering to please God on some matter, but fear bars the way. Try Mary's phrase . . . and rejoice in the glorious impossibility of it all.

> GOD'S EVERY ACT
> IS A POINT OF
> WONDER FOR
> THOSE HE CALLS
> TO PARTICIPATE
> IN IT.

# AN ADDITIONAL READING

*Read: Judges 7:9-15*

Gideon's story is another one—like Mary's—fraught with all the puzzling impossibilities of God's plan. Though his army was few in number, though his own nature was more the coward than the captain, Gideon discovered that God would do all He said . . . any way He wanted to do it. He can do it with clay pots and trumpets. Or a poor virgin girl. Or you. Or me. Or anything.

## PRAYER

*Lord,* I have never been more exhilarated than when I have found myself doing the impossible. Help me to say the next time I am afraid, "Consider me the Lord's slave." Let me remember Mary's example and say "yes"—then stand back and enjoy the ride.

# DECEMBER 9

*When* Elizabeth heard Mary's greeting, the baby leaped inside her, and Elizabeth was filled with the Holy Spirit. Then she exclaimed with a loud cry: "Blessed are you among women, and blessed is your offspring!"

LUKE 1:41-42

# BLESSED!

Life! What a wonderful word! The Incarnation! What a blessed doctrine! How glorious of God, who is everlasting Spirit, to put Himself at risk—to make His hazardous journey into flesh. Taking on the bulky flesh of humanity, He affirmed every person whom He touched. No idea is so essential to our hope as that which teaches that God was in Christ reconciling the world unto Himself.

Consider these two ordinary women, Mary and Elizabeth. These wonderful and fragile creatures were the means by which God became a human being. Thus, they shared a heavy secret. One of them was so old she was well past the childbearing age. She stood with one foot in the grave

> FIND THOSE WHO CARRY SOME HEAVY PLAN OF GOD, AND BLESS THEM FOR THEIR YIELDEDNESS.

and the other in the neonatal ward. Elizabeth must have found her joyous, old-age pregnancy the brunt of community gossip. Then her young friend from the north came to visit her. Mary affirmed Elizabeth in her commitment to God. No one but Mary could really understand and identify with

Elizabeth. Why? She too was the object of community ridicule back in Nazareth.

Each of the women had been asked to bear a heavy load, yet each of them helped the other with their respective assignments. Each had a special gift with which to help the other along. This wonderful gift is one that works in every situation. *It is the gift of affirmation.*

Mary, no doubt, had been struggling with her heavy assignment. She must bear the Son of God. Yet she could not tell her story and receive any satisfaction. She had to face Isaiah's words again and again: "Who has believed our report? And to whom has the arm of the LORD been revealed?" (Isaiah 53:1). No one would believe she could have a child without a human father. So she lived alone, glad to serve God, but desperate for even one other person to believe her.

Then Elizabeth greeted her, "Blessed are you!" In the power of such a kind affirmation, Mary could live and thrive and serve God.

Are you an Elizabeth? Can you offer a kind word to those who carry a heavy burden? Can you say, "Blessed are you!" to someone who is hurting? Perhaps this is the most Christlike ministry of all: to be able to say to the desperate, who are often isolated by their unbearable pain, "Blessed are you!"

# AN ADDITIONAL READING

*Read: Luke 6:20-23*

Poverty. Hunger. Tears. Exclusion. They are the temporary domain of the faithful, the wilderness of those obediently making their way to glory. But God has riches for them. Food. Comfort. Acceptance. It often comes in the form of friends like you who take time for a cup of coffee, create space in an overcrowded schedule, and make eye contact with those so beaten down they cannot face their fearful world.

## PRAYER

*Lord,* are my eyes open to those around me who may be carrying a load so heavy that they are being crushed? I wonder if I have passed people in such pain and been irresponsible with my "blessed-are-you's." Forgive me when I have not loved and encouraged the broken with a healing hope.

# DECEMBER 10

*Mary said: "My soul proclaims the greatness of the Lord, and my spirit has rejoiced in God my Savior, because He has looked with favor on the humble condition of His slave. Surely, from now on all generations will call me blessed, because the Mighty One has done great things for me, and holy is His name."* LUKE 1:46-49

# THE WAY BACK TO JOY

How Mary must have longed to understand her inscrutable God. How often her monster-sized doubts must have terrorized her. How could she do all of the will of God and not be destroyed by it?

But let Mary teach you the way to joy. When the burdens of life are too much for you, when your tears know no encouragement, do not see this as a suffering that has come only to you. Read the Scriptures and you will see that nearly all of God's servants have suffered from depression. Men and women throughout history have felt the ugly talons of despair sink deeply into their souls, enduring a spiritual depression that can rarely be shaken off by intention alone.

But there is a way to beat this despair. Let Mary teach it to you.

*Give yourself to the art of praise.*

Mary learned that there is really only one way to deal with spiritual or psychological depression, one sure way to forget your grief: exalt the Lord. It is a wonder that in praising Him, we drive back the demons of self-pity.

We cannot focus on His greatness and our depression at the same time. If we remain focused on how bad we feel, we will be unable to concentrate on the Savior. But focus on His greatness and you will find it impossible to dwell on your own painful circumstances.

*"My soul proclaims the greatness of the Lord, and my spirit rejoices in God my Savior."* Whatever Mary's emotional state was as she began her praise, it must surely have reached an exalted mood by the time she finished it. So it is with praise. Let it sweep the gloom from your heart and replace it with the joy that comes from adoration.

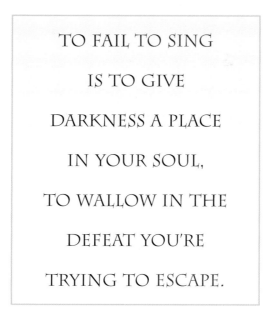

TO FAIL TO SING

IS TO GIVE

DARKNESS A PLACE

IN YOUR SOUL,

TO WALLOW IN THE

DEFEAT YOU'RE

TRYING TO ESCAPE.

# AN ADDITIONAL READING

*Read: Psalm 73:13-28*

Sometimes this Christianity—and its call for self-sacrifice —seems counter-productive. The rest of the world seems to be piling their shopping carts higher than ours, enjoying themselves as much or more than we are this season—with no need to honor self-denial. But never despair! Let them stack their so-called blessings as high as the sky, and our God will always be for us a better, richer abundance.

## PRAYER

*Lord,* I give my grief to a better focus. I will surrender my depression to own the riches of praise. I will exalt Your name until the power of this joy drives desperation from my soul.

# DECEMBER 11

*"He has done a mighty deed with His arm; He has scattered the proud because of the thoughts of their hearts; He has toppled the mighty from their thrones and exalted the lowly. He has satisfied the hungry with good things and sent the rich away empty."*

LUKE 1:51-53

# THE TUNE OF THE UNKNOWNS

Mighty deeds are often the work of ordinary people. None of those whom we consider great Bible heroes were heroes to themselves. They were just ordinary people who collided with God during their walk of faith. Only then did their lives acquire superhero status.

Run down the list. Elijah, we are reminded, "was a man with a nature like ours" (James 5:17). So it was with Moses, who begged God to be released from his "liberator status." Jacob was so foolish as to wrestle with God. Job pleaded with God to kill him. Jonah ran from God. Peter denied Jesus. Thomas doubted Him. All in all, these men and women of Scripture—at least in their own eyes—were not the super-saints that we have made them out to be.

The simple hill girl named Mary certainly did not see herself as an almighty saint but only as a person of lowly status. God was the great One. Only He was mighty, exalting those of low degree.

Most of the great Bible heroes would have been surprised to look down from heaven and see how venerated they became. Perhaps no one would have been more surprised than Mary. How she must have trembled before the Almighty's request of her. She was reluctant to agree to God's plan. His will was not only hard to bear but impossible to explain to others. But the greatness of her life is that she did it. She didn't wait until God's plan was complete before she rejoiced. She sang her Magnificat from the very first moments she yielded her life to God.

You will find that you do not have to complete all that God has for you to do in order to find your own joy. From the moment you agree to yield your life, the glory will begin to flow. From that wonderful "yes" moment when you throw your reluctance overboard, you will begin to feel praise welling up in your life. You have only to praise Him to see the great possibilities of God, and they will be fully accomplished through you.

THE HIGH AND MIGHTY

RARELY SEEK GOD'S HELP,

SO MOST OF HIS WORK

IS DONE BY THOSE WITH

LESS REPUTATION.

## AN ADDITIONAL READING

*Read: Zechariah 4:1-10*

The work of God in the hands of an ordinary you or me is a living picture of God's grace and glory—His grace, in that He invests Himself in one so frail and faulty; His glory, in that He creates real art with such raw clay. Are you at the end of your own strength? Have you bottomed out on self-confidence? Trust. Wait. Behold what wonders can be done through you by the Spirit of the living God!

## PRAYER

*Lord,* You exalt the humble. You use the yielded. Help me not to feel that I am worthy or deserving of You. Help me not to think I can do anything major with minor trust. Help me to say "yes" to Your every proposition so I can sing with Mary, "My soul proclaims the greatness of the Lord."

# DECEMBER 12

*"You, child, will be called a prophet of the Most High, for you will go before the Lord to prepare His ways, to give His people knowledge of salvation through the forgiveness of their sins, because of our God's merciful compassion by which the Dawn from on high will visit us, to shine on those who live in darkness and the shadow of death, to guide our feet into the way of peace."* LUKE 1:76-79

# BORN FOR GREATER PURPOSES

Here and there, old men sing! God took the aged patriarch, Zachariah, and magnified his joy. Look—the timeless old man suddenly has a lullaby. See him as he holds his baby in his weathered, old hands—the son he had obediently named John instead of Junior. Hear his old throat sing: *"You, child, will be called a prophet of the Most High."* A father may be grandiose with such a lullaby, but Zachariah was not. His little boy was a promised world changer.

• *"For you will go before the Lord to prepare His ways."* This is a sweet tribute to the Lord whom his son would one day introduce. At the moment of Zachariah's lullaby, his son's unborn Lord was still in Mary's womb. But Jesus was on the way! These two little babies—Jesus and John—were set for the rise and fall of many in Israel and, indeed, for people throughout out the world in all the ages yet to come.

MOST PARENTS HOLD ON TO THEIR CHILDREN TOO TIGHTLY. ZACHARIAH SET HIS FREE TO SERVE WHATEVER USE GOD HAD FOR HIM.

- *"To give His people knowledge of salvation."* The old man's lullaby admitted that the human race was plagued by feelings of lostness. Only the Good News which revealed that God was in Christ reconciling the world to Himself could take away this lost feeling.

- *"To shine on those who live in darkness and the shadow of death."* The world is a cold place where it is difficult to find light and warmth. The old man's lullaby was more honest than poetic. So many people are lost. So many live in the shadow of death. This little baby would bring light to all people. Those in the cold, dark shadow of death would be able to overcome death.

- *"To guide our feet in the way of peace."* Peace is the word that Jesus and John would bring to a world at war. The words of Jesus and John have not been able to call a halt to conflicts; there have been as many wars waged since they came as there were before. Still, they proclaimed an inner peace that even people at war could rely on. Jesus and John would release the world from turmoil.

Let an old man's lullaby become your song—your tribute to the One who entered the human arena on your behalf. Praise Him who is the way of salvation, the pathway to peace.

# AN ADDITIONAL READING

*Read: Psalm 51:10-17*

We are not required to have ten years of right answers or perfect church attendance in order to declare Jesus Christ to those around us. In fact, the power of God shines brightest when seen against our weakness. Let Him make your life fruitful despite your seasons of fruitlessness. Be an open book where others read of God's promises.

# PRAYER

*Lord,* come to me with peace. Remind me that Your purpose was to cleanse me of turmoil and prepare my heart for Your salvation. Open my mouth to show others Your way.

# DECEMBER 13

*The birth of Jesus Christ came about this way: After His mother Mary had been engaged to Joseph, before they came together, she was found to be with child by the Holy Spirit. So Joseph, her husband, being a righteous man, and not wanting to disgrace her publicly, decided to divorce her secretly.*

JOHN 16:8

# HOW TO HANDLE A SCANDAL

The birth of Jesus is the central majesty of history. The Resurrection validated all His claims, but His birth began this healing drama. His coming to earth through the womb of a virgin was a most strategic miracle. God invaded history, and His invasion came as an all-pervasive miracle that plunged the world into significance.

But even great events can disturb the tranquility of those who are God's partners in a miracle.

The first to confront the virgin birth was Mary's fiancé, Joseph. He could in no way understand why Mary called it a miracle when the rest of the world saw it as adultery. Joseph was disturbed by Mary's pregnancy, for he thought it was an evident case of infidelity. He wanted to get Mary out of town quietly. He loved her too much to consider humiliating her with a rude, public exposure. Rather, he planned to "put her away" in such a manner as to protect her from those who might want to stone her as an adulteress.

*Let the heart of Joseph teach you how to avoid a vindictive spirit.*

Along the pathway of your pilgrimage, you will meet those who appear to be guilty of some kind of unforgivable fault. When you meet them, adopt the spirit of Joseph. Remember when you hear such people being criticized that no person is beyond the love of God. Those who are clearly outcasts should still be loved.

> THE HOLY VIRGIN BIRTH IS HARD ON THOSE WHO WANT TO CLING TO NATURAL, EXPLAINABLE THINGS.

Sometimes your loving treatment of the guilty may actually awaken a change in their lives. From that awakening may come reform or maybe even usefulness to God. Still, in some cases you may never see this transformation. Kind treatment cannot always change an evil nature. But your kindness, even toward those who are rogues, will be an indication that you are striving toward Christlikeness.

Do not forget that Jesus was kind even to a dying thief. Seek to make such compassion yours.

## AN ADDITIONAL READING

*Read: Acts 9:19-31*

Sometimes those who are the subject of scorn and scandal are merely misunderstood. And if someone would just take a minute to listen without judging and ask questions without condemning, they might see a person who is a lot more than fodder for the gossip mill. Is there someone in your life who could have an easier time living for Christ if they didn't have such a hard time getting other Christians to love them?

## PRAYER

*Lord,* how much I need to remember this line from the Lord's Prayer: "Forgive us our debts, as we also have forgiven our debtors." Then maybe I can look at those who stand publicly accused and remember that Satan was my accuser before I first experienced Your forgiveness.

# DECEMBER 14

*After he had considered these things, an angel of the Lord suddenly appeared to him in a dream, saying, "Joseph, son of David, don't be afraid to take Mary as your wife, because what has been conceived in her is by the Holy Spirit. She will give birth to a son, and you are to name Him Jesus, because He will save His people from their sins."*

MATTHEW 1:20-21

# PART OF THE PLAN

Just when Joseph was despairing over what he thought was Mary's unfaithfulness, he had an angelic visitation of his own. And this intrusive angel did a wonderful thing: he included Joseph in the great plan of God. God has a way of taking even critical bystanders and including them in His universal plan.

God asked Joseph to do two things:

• *First, he was told to marry Mary.* Joseph must have greeted the news that Mary was chaste and pure with great joy. With even greater joy, he heard God's command to go ahead with his plans to marry.

• *Second, he was instructed to name the baby.* The task of naming the baby was given to Joseph, even though he was not the natural father of Jesus. He was to name the baby Yeshua, or "God delivers." God had made it clear: this baby would grow up to be the Savior. Joseph would not only name the child but give the world this promise: Jesus would save His people from their sins.

Nothing is more glorious than being included in the work of God. Joseph went from the despondency of being critical of Mary to the glory of being involved with her in all that God wanted done.

*Is this not a great lesson for us?* So often in church, those who cause problems may be doing so because they feel they are not a part of what is going on. The way to sweeten such sour discord is to widen the involvement. Take those critical observers and put them on the task force that serves the dreams of God. Many people who become destructive in their moods are just waiting for someone to say, "Would you mind giving us a hand?"

Joseph married Mary by divine command, and he named Jesus by divine command. When God orders our participation in anything—whether it be something as grand as the Incarnation or as simple as serving in the church—we are made valuable both in our own eyes and in the eyes of the world.

THE PROUD CARPENTER CEASED CARING ABOUT WHAT WAS PROPER AND BEGAN TO CARE ABOUT WHAT WAS RIGHT.

# AN ADDITIONAL READING

*Read: Ephesians 2:12-22*

We live in an age that has lost so much of the sense of community. Remember when we used to bake pies for new neighbors? Where went those Saturdays spent helping others? How much more fulfilling would your Christian life be if you suddenly recaptured the camaraderie of some common cause, the freedom of seeking His kingdom with others who share your Savior?

# PRAYER

*Lord,* grace has saved me and placed me in the bosom of love forever. I must thank You for this grace that gave me something to do in the kingdom of God. I am also grateful for my strategic importance in all that You are trying to accomplish in the world.

# DECEMBER 15

$\mathcal{N}$ow all this took place to fulfill what was spoken by the Lord through the prophet: "See, the virgin will be with child and give birth to a son, and they will name Him Immanuel, which is translated 'God is with us.'"

MATTHEW 1:22-23

# GOD IS WITH US

The word *Immanuel* is second only to the word *Lord* in Christian worship. *Incarnation* is the way theologians say *Immanuel*. The Incarnation is the noblest idea of any world religion. God did not watch human despair from the safety of heaven. He clothed himself in humanity. He ceased watching the human war and became a soldier. Oh, the things that God experienced in becoming a man:

> DID GOD
>
> TRY TO
>
> BECOME
>
> A MAN?
>
> NO.
>
> GOD
>
> NEVER
>
> TRIED
>
> ANYTHING.
>
> HE DID IT.

- the blistering summer sun,
- the shivering rains of winter,
- the blight of hunger when He fasted after His baptism,
- the desperation of bereavement when His earthly father died,
- the empathy of a mother's tears when she stood at the cross,
- the disappearance of all friends at His arrest in Gethsemane,
- the pain of a friend's denials when Peter quaked before the truth,
- the staggering shock of treachery by His friend Judas,
- the horror of naked judgment with no one to speak on His behalf,

- the agony of crucifixion where He experienced the status of a convict,
- the agony of death,
- the loneliness of being forsaken by everyone.

All these things—when put together—spell *Immanuel.* These things are what the God of all mercy took upon Himself.

But why did He do it? Because these sorts of things form the fabric of all of our living. We cannot live without bumps and pains, without heartache and desolation, without mosquito bites and cancer. Immanuel was God saying, "You shall not bear such pain alone." God became flesh to redeem.

Let Jesus be incarnate in your life, and then maybe when you have stooped to serve the desperate and dying, you will hear them say the word *Immanuel.* When Christ becomes incarnate in your life, you will hear those you serve saying to you, "I cannot help but believe in Christ. I have seen Him in your life."

# AN ADDITIONAL READING

*Read: First Corinthians 2:1-5*

How much convincing does it really take to share with someone the blessings of Christmas? The world rarely responds to our profound arguments. It is rarely moved by our wise perspectives, even when we present them well. It is more often won by our thoughtfulness than our theology. It is more often drawn to God by His presence in our lives than by our persuasion. It is our Christ, not our creed, which captures people's hearts.

## PRAYER

*Lord,* make me an instrument of Your incarnation. Live in me until my life is so submerged in Yours that I am invisible. Wherever I go, whatever I do, may I hear those around me breathe the word *Immanuel,* suggesting that I am nothing and You are everything.

# DECEMBER 16

*Joseph also went up from the town of Nazareth in Galilee, to Judea, to the city of David, which is called Bethlehem, because he was of the house and family line of David, to be registered along with Mary, who was engaged to him and was pregnant. While they were there, it happened that the days were completed for her to give birth. Then she gave birth to her firstborn Son, and she wrapped Him snugly in cloth and laid Him in a manger—because there was no room for them at the inn.* LUKE 2:4-7

# THE OUT BACK

Bethlehem! A crowded and inhospitable little city! On that night of nights, a quiet, disturbing event took place in the fields near the shepherd's cave. The town—for at least a decade or two—never knew that God had come and gone in a shepherd's cave behind a rustic inn.

*Is this not a lesson on the subtlety of God's greatness?* We often look for Him in the roar and the trumpet, in the earthquake and the fire. Then we discover that He came to earth in a way that was most beautiful: He walked through our midst in felted fields and whispered to a few people that He was in the neighborhood. So it was at Bethlehem.

The plot of God's visitation has several prominent elements:

• Mary, fatigued by travel and the contractions of childbirth, was so much in pain that she was willing to lie down anywhere.

• Joseph, worn out by village refusals, was willing to take even a stable for the birth of his son.

• The baby, the central character of this drama, found the evening just right to begin that celebration of celebrations we would later call so tenderly . . . Christmas.

And so it happened. Mary, supported by her good husband, gave birth to Jesus. Then she wrapped Him in strips of cloth against the cold of the night.

He was God, this baby! It was easy to tell that, for so the angels sang that night. But He was also fully human. The infant wept. He snuggled against Mary's breast and drank of the life that mothers ever hold for their little ones. This was the grandest warmth of Jesus entering our world: the infinite God whimpering for milk in a shepherd's cave.

Most of Bethlehem didn't know God was in town. Some people there may still not know it or at least not think much of it. Sometimes God comes so quietly, you have to listen closely to know He's even there.

GOD OFTEN ARRIVES INCOGNITO AND EMBARRASSES THE SELFISH WHO HAVE DENIED HIM A PLACE TO STAY.

# AN ADDITIONAL READING

*Read: Psalm 5:1-7*

We struggle to find answers to our problems. *Where are You, God?* We feel trapped in the grip of our circumstances. *Lord, where have You gone?* We are blamed for things we didn't do. *God, haven't You anything to say about this?* Take heart! We are not alone in our search for God. Despair not! God is here this morning . . . this noon . . . this night . . . whenever, wherever, whatever we happen to be doing.

# PRAYER

*Lord,* sometimes You come quietly and with no disturbance. Babies threaten no one, and no memorials are raised to mark their significance. May my life bring Christ quietly into the circle of human need so those who need You will not be frightened by Your presence but enveloped in it.

# DECEMBER 17

*In the same region, shepherds were living out in the fields and keeping watch at night over their flock. Then an angel of the Lord stood before them, and the glory of the Lord shone around them, and they were terrified. But the angel said to them, "Do not be afraid, for you see, I announce to you good news of great joy that will be for all the people: because today in the city of David was born for you a Savior, who is Christ the Lord."* LUKE 2:8-11

# HIGH DRAMA ON A HILLSIDE

Isaiah had predicted it eight centuries earlier: "The Spirit of the Lord GOD is upon me, because the LORD has anointed me to bring good news to the afflicted. He has sent me to bind up the brokenhearted, to proclaim liberty to the captives, and release to the prisoners" (Isaiah 61:1). How odd that some rustic field hands were the first to get the news.

How wonderful it is when the poor get good news. Good news more often comes to the rich. But upon this dramatic, exceptional night, the poor got the news first. The rich did not even suspect it.

The old carol "Good Christian Men Rejoice" celebrates the shepherds' joy that night with these unforgettable words:

*Good Christian men, rejoice,*
*With heart and soul and voice.*
*Give ye heed to what we say.*
*News! News!*
*Jesus Christ is born today.*
*Ox and ass before Him bow,*
*And He is in the manger now.*
*Christ is born today!*
*Christ is born today!*

This was news made especially for the poor! So they came, these country shepherds— these to whom the angels had announced the Savior.

This Jesus—said the angels— would take away their sins. This was, indeed, good news! Poor people have no more sins than the rich, but they are less schooled in social smugness, so they are often more honest about their sins.

Isn't Jesus' coming good news to you as well? Remember how you felt when you realized that the Savior had come to deal with your sins? Didn't it feel good when you let Him do it?

> THIS BABY WAS TOO SPECIAL TO BE ANNOUNCED IN ORDINARY WAYS. GET INTO TOWN AND FALL ON YOUR KNEES.

## AN ADDITIONAL READING

*Read: Luke 7:40-47*

Self-esteem may be overvalued unless it looks into the window of God's glory and sees the treasures of eternity, marked *Free for the Asking*. When we are too satisfied with our own significance, we cannot see how our self-esteem melts before the majesty of God's love and mercy. Let the dignity of Christ bring to you the purest form of significance.

## PRAYER

*Lord,* how great was the news that night in Bethlehem. How gladly the poor in spirit still receive that news. How wonderfully the news changes life. Help me to love the Good News and to be a better newsboy than I have been.

# DECEMBER 18

*Suddenly there was a multitude of the heavenly host with the angel, praising God and saying: "Glory to God in the highest heaven, and peace on earth to people He favors!" When the angels had left them and returned to heaven, the shepherds said to one another, "Let's go straight to Bethlehem and see this thing that has taken place, which the Lord has made known to us."* LUKE 2:13-15

# THE HIGHEST GLORY

The glory of the revelation of God! How wonderful it is when God draws the drapes on some hidden part of His glory and lets the incandescence of heaven flood in! That is what the word *revelation* means: "to disclose, to bring into openness things once hidden."

Revelation does not occur because we are able to tear something of God's hidden splendor away from Him. Revelation is all of God; it happens only when He decides to disclose Himself to us, to let us in on His glory.

This is what happened that night in the fields near Bethlehem. God split the skies and let the angels declare His glory to a band of frightened field hands.

*How did they receive His glory?* When God discloses Himself, at first there is awe . . . then fear . . . then astonishment . . . and finally joy. Revelation is a kind of insight that sweeps over us all at once. It hits us like unshielded light, illuminating the center of our existence. Truths that were once dark and obscure burst from the mist. We see them and are overwhelmed by their glory. Then the hidden things of God impact and change us.

So Jesus longs to give you more insights than you can have through your own personal Bible study or mechanical disciplines. Who gets this glorious revelation? Those who are hungry for light. So it came to the shepherds: "Today in the city of David was born for you a Savior, who is Christ the Lord." Not revelation enough? Then there is more: "He will save His people from their sins." There is still more revelation; listen to this: "Glory to God in the highest heaven, and peace on earth to people He favors!"

What happened after that? Were they still shepherds? Yes. And no. They were still shepherds, but not the same shepherds. In fact, they would never be the same shepherds again! Once God shows you His glory, you have a new standard of life by which all later values must be forever measured.

DOES NOT THE JOY OF CHRIST'S COMING WAKE YOU AT MIDNIGHT WITH GRATITUDE?

# AN ADDITIONAL READING

*Read: Revelation 1:12-18*

Standing before our poor institutional gods, we too often find ourselves fighting back a yawn, taking note of how so-and-so is wearing her hair now, or checking our watches to see how long it is till lunch. But the shepherds—like the Apostle John in this passage—could not stand before Christ. They were too awed. They could only fall to the ground, praising God from a prone position. Wouldn't you love to recapture the wonder, to get weak in the knees at the sound of your Savior's voice?

## PRAYER

*Lord,* reveal Yourself to me. If I am frightened by Your self-disclosure, at least allow me to see the message that transforms my littleness by encountering Your glory.

# DECEMBER 19

*They hurried off and found both Mary and Joseph, and the baby who was lying in the manger. After seeing them, they reported the message they were told about this child, and all who heard it were amazed at what the shepherds said to them. But Mary was treasuring up all these things in her heart and meditating on them.* LUKE 2:16-19

# THE HEART OF CHRISTMAS

Mary pondered all these things in her heart. What things? The wonderful season of Christ's coming.

These keepsakes were in Mary's heart years before a single Gospel had been written to record their significance. Pity! She did not know her tribute song that others further down the centuries would write:

*What child is this, who laid to rest*
*On Mary's lap is sleeping?*
*Whom angels greet with anthems sweet*
*While shepherds' watch are keeping.*
*This—this is Christ the King,*
*Whom shepherds guard and angels sing;*
*Haste! Haste to bring him laud—*
*The babe, the son of Mary!*

These for Mary were the laudable, ponderable keepsakes of her heart. The romance of that first Christmas settled down over every later Christmas. The créche continues talking back to all who are sensitive of soul.

We know that in the midst of this romantic tale lies a real story of deprivation and glory, of simplicity and splendor. A small woman, a small baby, the rags of poverty, the riches of salvation—all of these elements are woven so tightly into a single fabric that there is no sorting the warp from the woof. The only place where all of the majesty of that first Christmas with all its earth-shattering splendor could live was within the heart of a real woman in a real stable on a real night, making possible the real story of our salvation.

> THE HEART IS THAT SMALL, FLESHLY VAULT THAT HOLDS VAST TREASURES NONE CAN EVER TAKE AWAY.

Thus, we return to a crude manger each Christmas to look again at a story quickly told but never forgotten. Mary's pondering was contagious. Now the whole world ponders this glorious epoch of redemption.

# AN ADDITIONAL READING

*Read: Proverbs 4:20-23*

The years have a way of hardening our hearts, toughening them against disappointment, closeting off our dreams before they have a chance to backfire on us. But never forget Mary, who chose to keep her heart tender and open to God's glorious possibilities. Always keep the truths of God's Word sealed in your own heart. Those who cherish such promises are the first to notice them when they come to pass.

# PRAYER

*Lord,* my heart is empty when it might be full of splendor. May I make my heart a filing cabinet of Your visitation to my private planet, so I may ever celebrate the impact I must allow You to have in my life.

# DECEMBER 20

*W*hen the days of their purification according to the law of Moses were completed, they brought Him up to Jerusalem to present Him to the Lord (just as it is written in the law of the Lord: "Every firstborn male will be called holy to the Lord") and to offer a sacrifice (according to what is stated in the law of the Lord: a pair of turtledoves or two young pigeons).

LUKE 2:22-24

# COMING INTO A FORTUNE

Jesus the firstborn! The firstborn by law and God's heir to a kingdom! This Christ will inherit the universe, but He is not stingy with His inheritance: "I pray that the eyes of your heart may be enlightened," His servant tells us, "so you may know what is the hope of His calling, what are the glorious riches of His inheritance among the saints" (Ephesians 1:18).

Jesus the firstborn has made us joint heirs, testifies the apostle: "All those led by God's Spirit are God's sons. For you did not receive a spirit of slavery to fall back into fear, but you received the Spirit of adoption, by whom we cry out, 'Abba, Father!' The Spirit Himself testifies together with our spirit that we are God's children, and if children, also heirs—heirs of God and co-heirs with Christ—seeing that we suffer with Him so that we may also be glorified with Him" (Romans 8:14-17).

We are indeed partakers in this firstborn status of Christ. Mary and Joseph offered two turtledoves for the consecration of their firstborn. If we are joint heirs with Christ, should we not also be looking for our own acceptable offering to confirm our heritage this holiday season?

Christmas is a season of gifts. God is lavish in giving us all things. Eternity itself is our gift! Who can say exactly all that we shall inherit? We do know this: "The sufferings of this present time are not worth comparing with the glory that is going to be revealed to us. . . . And not only that, but we ourselves who have the Spirit as the firstfruits—we also groan within ourselves, eagerly waiting for adoption, the redemption of our bodies" (Romans 8:18,23). This is the proof that our heritage will be glorious, for "what no eye has seen and no ear has heard, and what has never come into a man's heart, is what God has prepared for those who love Him" (1 Corinthians 2:9).

We are indeed Christmas participants in our firstborn status in Jesus Christ. All that is His is ours. All that He has given us leads us to cry, "Hallelujah! The inheritance ahead of us is all of grace!"

> WE WHO HAVE BEEN ADOPTED INTO GOD'S FAMILY ARE MADE RICH WITH HIS GIFTS.

# AN ADDITIONAL READING

*Read: Galatians 4:4-7*

The Scriptures are replete with the news: we are the children of God, heirs according to the promise. We don't deserve it; we merely accept it. We must never think we've earned it, yet we needn't cower before its grandeur. Like fathers who delight to see their children unwrapping their presents around the Christmas tree, our Lord thrills to see us enjoying His gifts, embracing the joy of our Father's inheritance.

# PRAYER

*Lord*, when Mary offered the doves in celebration of the status of her firstborn Son, did she know she was passing that status on to all who would receive her Son?

Hallelujah! My inheritance is forever sealed in Your all-inclusive grace.

# DECEMBER 21

*W*hen the parents brought in the child Jesus to perform for Him what was customary under the law, Simeon took Him up in his arms, praised God, and said: "Now, Master, You can dismiss Your slave in peace, according to Your word. For my eyes have seen Your salvation, which You have prepared in the presence of all peoples—a light for revelation to the Gentiles and glory to Your people Israel."

LUKE 2:27-32

# THE REWARDS OF WAITING

Simeon's long wait was over. He had managed to live just long enough to see the Messiah. Now he could be gathered to his fathers in great contentment. Can you see the grandeur of such a simple scene?

What kind of Messiah was Simeon expecting? One already shod with military might and valor? This was the picture that many people held; yet suddenly the infant God was in the temple, and Simeon was so sensitive to the call of God that he reached out his hands for the baby.

Then there was Mary. Did she hesitate as a new mother to hand her infant son to an old man? Did her motherly instincts want to forbid this stranger to touch her son? Maybe it was the light on the old man's face that made her surrender her little one without fear.

Then there were Simeon's grand words: "Now, Master, You can dismiss Your slave in peace, according to Your word. For my eyes have seen Your salvation, which You have prepared in the presence of all peoples—a light for revelation to the Gentiles and glory to Your people Israel."

Suddenly the light on the old man's brow seemed like a halo of God's concurrence. Yet there was no halo—not on Jesus, not on Simeon. Halos are the artists' work of later centuries. There was more of an ordinary mystique in this salutation.

Mary had no halo; Joseph had no halo. There were no angels singing, no choirs to accompany Simeon's declaration.

Isn't that just like God? He never uses special lighting or stage props. God came to old Simeon just as He always did, in the daily round—in the sixes and sevens of life. Here was a grand declaration void of showy grandeur. Its simplicity is in its profundity. Its glory resides in the fact that it could have happened on any ordinary day . . . as indeed it did.

Isn't that rather like the day Jesus declared Himself to you?

GOD

ALWAYS KEEPS

HIS WORD.

ALL THAT

HE SAYS,

HE WILL DO.

GREAT IS HIS

FAITHFULNESS.

## AN ADDITIONAL READING

*Read: Micah 7:1-7*

It's close to Christmas now. All moods are soft around the edges. Life seems little more than a picture postcard. But soon—too soon—the papers will once again read like the first six verses of this passage. That's why believers in Christ always need to read on to verse 7. For our hope is in God. And we can live through anything—no matter how dark and distasteful—knowing that one day, He will make every day feel like Christmas.

## PRAYER

*Lord,* I am grateful that Simeon was blessed by seeing the infant Messiah. He couldn't see exactly how Jesus would do His saving, but Simeon could see that He would do it. Now I have seen You. May the salvation that Simeon saw in the distance be as much of a glory in my life as it was in his.

# DECEMBER 22

*His father and mother were amazed at what was being said about Him. Then Simeon blessed them and told His mother Mary: "Indeed, this child is destined to cause the fall and rise of many in Israel, and to be a sign that will be opposed—and a sword will pierce your own soul—that the thoughts of many hearts may be revealed."* LUKE 2:33-35

# WHEN LOVE HURTS

Old Simeon had just pronounced a beautiful benediction on the infant Jesus. Why would his final words offer such gloom and doom to the young couple on such a sunny occasion? What could he mean—"a sword will pierce your own soul"?

It was the *word* that Simeon used for "sword" that so unnerved them. The Greek language had at least two different words for "sword." First, there was the *machaira,* the Roman infantry sword—a double-bladed sword very effective in Roman military maneuvers, but short and not very formidable. Simeon did not use this word, however. He used *rhomphaia,* the word for a long Persian weapon that resembled a skewer on which whole animals might be cooked over an open flame. What a horrible picture to a young mother!

Mary already knew *some* of the price she would have to pay for being the handmaid of the Lord. The pain she had endured before Jesus was born was immense. She probably had also endured the contempt of community gossips over a pregnancy out of wedlock. She had borne the momentary rejection of Joseph, who (for a while) had considered breaking their engagement and getting her out of town. She had persevered through the pain of a long trip to Bethlehem in the ninth month of her pregnancy, followed by another hard trip to exile in Egypt until she could return safely to Nazareth.

Old Simeon's prophecy told her that she would have to pay a terrible price on *both* ends of Jesus' life—a sword she could not fully imagine at this stage. Later on, she was surely among the women who followed Jesus along the Via Dolorosa to the cross (Luke 23:28). We know for certain that she was at Jesus' cross, for one of Christ's seven last words deals with His concern for His mother's welfare (John 19:26-27).

So what was Simeon saying to this mother and child? Just this: the day would come when her sweet little baby would become a man. He would then die, and Mary would be forced to grieve as few mothers have ever done. Mary would then taste what Paul said we must all learn—the "fellowship of His sufferings" (Philippians 3:10). All who look on Jesus' death without grieving have failed to understand that they—like Mary— are involved in the cross.

THE WILL OF GOD IS NEVER BARGAIN STUFF. DO NOT SING YOUR GLAD NOELS WITHOUT THINKING OF ALL THEY MEAN.

## AN ADDITIONAL READING

*Read: First Peter 4:12-19*

Even some of the joys of our Christmas experiences come at the cost of money, time, and long lines at the supermarket checkout. Yet throughout this season, let us rejoice! Nothing of value comes without some price, and the privilege of being related to Christ through His grace-filled bloodline may also come at some greater expense than we can now imagine. Christmas may bring you some trials of pain and separation. Yet swords can only cut so deep. And one day, like Mary, we will celebrate a victory no sword can ever take from us.

## PRAYER

*Lord,* Mary would have to live long enough to sorrow at the cross of her Son. Have I felt her pain? Do I care that You died and—most of all—do I care that You died for me? I know that I will never mature as a believer until it dawns on me that I am responsible for Your death. Surely at such a moment, a sword should pierce my own soul. May I care this much.

# DECEMBER 23

*After Jesus was born in Bethlehem of Judea in the days of King Herod, wise men from the east arrived unexpectedly in Jerusalem, saying, "Where is He who has been born King of the Jews? For we saw His star in the east and have come to worship Him." When King Herod heard this, he was deeply disturbed, and all Jerusalem with him. So he assembled all the chief priests and scribes of the people and asked them where the Messiah would be born.* MATTHEW 2:1-4

# SMALL TOWN SURPRISES

No doubt Herod was surprised that when God picked a city for the birth of His Son, He selected Bethlehem. It might have offended Herod that God would pick such a small, one-camel town. But what *really* offended him was that God didn't pick one of Herod's own sons to be the king of the Jews.

Shall we rebuke the magi for not picking a more politically sensitive word than "King"? Right off, Herod's sense of dynasty was offended. His own princes should be king after him, as he saw it. For the moment, Herod kept his cool and acted sincerely interested in where the "King of the Jews" would be born.

It was a day of surprises for Herod. A great king had been born without his knowledge. *How great a king can this be,* he must have reasoned, *if I didn't get a birth announcement?* Then to his even greater surprise, the baby was born in Bethlehem. *How big a thing can God get done in such a small place?* he must have wondered.

There is no end to God's use of places of insignificance. God never starts looking at city populations to determine where He will do some mighty work. He started the whole Jewish faith with Abraham of Ur. Ur? Yes, Ur.

He started the whole adventure of Christianity in Nazareth. Nazareth? Yes, Nazareth. Why Nazareth? Because there He found a woman who was completely yielded to His purpose for her life. Great works of God rarely start in big places. Rather, they start in small places—in some person with a big commitment. Of course, Herod could not understand the idea of finding big commitment in small places.

How big is your place?

More important . . . how big is your commitment?

THE COMEDY OF GOD
IS THE NEVER-ENDING LAUGHTER
OF DIVINE SURPRISE.

# AN ADDITIONAL READING

*Read: Micah 5:2-4*

The grand pronouncement of Bethlehem's place in history was first given in this obscure couple of paragraphs from Micah's prophecy. It tells of a place that is small (like we are), of a place outshined by its divine resident (like we are), of a place that owes its peace and security (like ours does) to One who calls this place home. Are we really so small and unimportant? It depends on our commitment to find a noble place in His will.

## PRAYER

*Lord,* some of us are from pretty small towns. I know You don't mind. Really, I don't either. Help my submission to You to be bigger than my own insignificant zip code.

# DECEMBER 24

*Herod secretly summoned the wise men and learned from them the time when the star appeared. He sent them to Bethlehem and said, "Go and search carefully for the child. When you find Him, report back to me so that I too can go and worship Him."*  MATTHEW 2:7-8

# WORSHIP THE KING

How glorious the Christmas story might have been if Herod had really meant what he said. If Herod had fallen down and begun to worship the infant King, his whole future would have been glorious. But he didn't. He had no appetite for worship, no hunger for the divine visitation of God.

The kingdom of God has long thrived on those who have a desire to worship and adore. Yet we so easily grow devious in this business of worship, especially at Christmas. Christmas is a season of high worship attendance. Everyone goes to church at this holy season. But are not their hearts distracted? Are their minds clearly focused on the Son of God?

The glitzy materialism that has come to characterize Christmas makes Herods of us all. We may pretend to show interest in the Savior, but the season comes upon us like a frenzied neurosis, a materialism of fury. We "shop till we drop." We see a hundred secular television Christmas movies for every one we see about Jesus. We spend and spend and spend. As Wordsworth said in his "Composed on Westminster Bridge"—

*"Buying and spending, we lay waste our powers."*

Who could be king to Herod? Herod did not want to have a king; he wanted to be one. He did not really want to have a God; he wanted to be a god. Can this be said of us at Christmas?

It may be that the infant Christ has been replaced by our secular adoration at Christmas. The créche is too much in the way of the shopping mall to get our serious attention in December.

It has been said that anything which is more important than God to us is our god. Herod already had a god. It brought him little joy, but he was the only god he had time for, and thus he worshiped at a very low altar—the altar of his own ego.

COME LIKE THE MAGI—AND NOT LIKE HEROD—TO LOSE YOURSELF IN ADORATION.

What God crowns your altar this Christmas Eve? Where do you worship? Whom do you worship? A baby was born, and He came to change your destiny. He was given to you so your worship might rise higher than the adoration of your own materialistic ego.

Serve that baby, who after He became a man said, "If anyone wants to come with Me, he must deny himself, take up his cross, and follow Me" (Matthew 16:24).

## AN ADDITIONAL READING

*Read: Psalm 138:1-5*

Why not open up right now with a level of worship and praise Herod never found? He missed much by not knowing this feeling, this freedom, this festival we own and get to enjoy. On this day—this wonderful day—this expectant day before the most extraordinary of days—let us roll out our long list of reasons for thanksgiving, and give our praise a welcome place for the King of kings.

## PRAYER

*Lord,* Herod never wanted to worship, only to kill the infant Christ. I have never wanted to do that, of course, but does my adoration flag a bit at Christmas? Am I too captive to buying and spending to be captivated by the King of kings and Lord of lords? Raise Your great sacrifice high above the tinsel and glitter of my holidays. Let me see You high and lifted up. Let me look and live and worship You this Christmas.

# DECEMBER 25

*W*hen they saw the star, they were overjoyed beyond measure. Entering the house, they saw the child with Mary His mother, and falling to their knees, they worshiped Him. Then they opened their treasures and presented Him with gifts: gold, frankincense, and myrrh.     MATTHEW 2:10-11

# THE WORSHIP OF WISE MEN

Their gifts were three. We don't know their number for sure. Tradition indicates there were probably three wise men because of these three gifts. Tradition also has assigned names to these wise men: Caspar, Balthazar, and Melchior. We don't really know that they had camels, but apparently they crossed the desert. And camels were good for that sort of thing.

One thing we know for sure, though. They did bring three gifts. Consider their three gifts from that wonderful old Christmas legend that confronts us this time of year.

Consider first the testimony of the wise man who brought the gold:

> *Born a king of Bethlehem's plain.*
> *Gold I bring to crown him again;*
> *King forever, ceasing never,*
> *Over us all to reign.*

Consider next the words of him who brought the frankincense:

> *Frankincense to offer have I;*
> *Incense owns a deity nigh;*
> *Prayer and praising, all men raising,*
> *Worship him, God most high.*

Finally, consider the counsel of him who brought the myrrh:

*Myrrh is mine; its bitter perfume*

*Breathes a life of gathering gloom;*

*Sorrowing, sighing, bleeding, dying;*

*Sealed in a stone-cold tomb.*

Now hear them all as they offer the infant Jesus their worship:

*Glorious now behold him arise.*

*King and God and Sacrifice!*

*Heaven sings "Alleluia,"*

*"Alleluia," the earth replies!*

Do you have a little gold you might give Him this Christmas? Then offer it to Him. No frankincense? No myrrh? The best gifts you can offer Him are your hallelujahs. Worship and adore Him with all your heart.

> ALL OUR GIFTS
>
> ARE NOTHING COMPARED
>
> WITH THE TREASURE
>
> OF OUR HONEST WORSHIP.

# AN ADDITIONAL READING

*Read: Psalm 16:5-11*

Today we hold in our hands . . . a new shirt, maybe? A slick kitchen gadget? Shaving accessories? Perfume? Perhaps a bit of chocolate? At their heart, these things are not just merchandise; they are reminders that we matter to someone—someone who loves us enough to take an out-of-the-way trip and buy a gift just for us. Today, your best gift should be to want to be near God. Not to be in love with Christmas but in love with Christ.

## PRAYER

*Lord,* here's my adoration. It is the gift that honors You even as it keeps me alive. If there is no praise, there is no Christmas. Here are my hallelujahs. They are Yours, offered gladly from my own small but jubilant heart.

# DECEMBER 26

*The boy grew up and became strong, filled with wisdom, and God's grace was on Him. . . . And Jesus increased in wisdom and stature, and in favor with God and with people.*

LUKE 2:40,52

# THE CHRIST CHILD GROWS UP

Jesus' maturity was a matter of growing in four ways: in wisdom, in stature, and in favor with God and man. This means that Jesus' life expressed a hungering to get wiser, bigger, and better at relationships—both His relationship with His Father in heaven and His relationships with those around Him. Let us examine these four areas of maturity:

- *First, Jesus grew in wisdom.* His desire to be wise may have resulted in the simple wisdom that continues to astound the world. The heart of Jesus' wisdom gathers itself around the Sermon on the Mount. In this most famous sermon ever preached, the appeal is not to get smarter as a Ph.D. might, but to learn the lessons of the lilies, the birds, the wise and foolish builders. At the end of

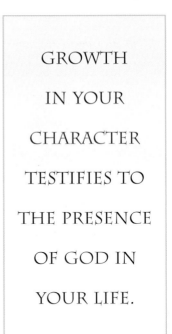

GROWTH IN YOUR CHARACTER TESTIFIES TO THE PRESENCE OF GOD IN YOUR LIFE.

this sermon, Matthew makes this comment: "When Jesus had finished this sermon, the crowds were astonished at His teaching. For He was teaching them like one who had authority, and not like their scribes" (Matthew 7:28-29).

- *Jesus also grew in stature.* What baby does not want to be a child? What child does not want to be an adolescent? What adolescent does not long to be a man or a woman? There can be no doubt that Jesus wanted to grow up. One very famous psychologist said that many people become full grown in their bodies but remain adolescent in their temperaments all their lives. Not so with Jesus; He matured in every way.

- *He also grew in favor with God.* Jesus had a longing to know God and to be with God. His prayer life reflected His appetite to be one with God. He walked and talked with God so that His bonding with His Father would be a growing and dependent relationship. He knew God to be His Father, and He passed this glorious "Abba" word on to the rest of us.

- *Finally, Jesus grew in favor with people.* He liked people, both those who liked Him and those who didn't. He wanted all people to be saved. No one was beyond the scope of His desire to love. He reached from the cross to prove He was the greatest person who ever lived.

Jesus considered maturity the business of every believer. Do you? Are you growing in wisdom and in your love affair with God and humanity?

# AN ADDITIONAL READING

*Read: Colossians 2:6-10*

It has been well said that people's inner lives never stand still. We are either making progress toward maturity or retreating toward sin and self-centeredness. At this time of year, we are inclined to look back over a sea of yesterdays. We can see the strides we've made as well as our past mistakes. There's more ground to cover, of course, and God has new ways to stretch us. Still, for today, take note of the progress God can produce from a yielded heart.

## PRAYER

*Lord,* I want to grow. I never want to stop growing! I want my maturity to be a gift that I give You to make You as attractive as I can to others—to make Your influence optimal in my minimal world.

# DECEMBER 27

*Every year His parents traveled to Jerusalem for the Passover Festival. When He was 12 years old, they went up according to the custom of the festival. After those days were over, as they were returning, the boy Jesus stayed behind in Jerusalem, but His parents did not know it. Assuming He was in the traveling party, they went a day's journey. Then they began looking for Him among their relatives and friends.*

LUKE 2:41-44

# LOOSE IN THE TEMPLE

This holiday season is drawing to a close, but let us not allow it to go without seeing it as a season of family and all that the word *family* means to us. Let us come to the Holy Family and seek their definition of family, learning how to love and raise our children.

Mary and Joseph likely took Jesus to the temple in Jerusalem every year. They could never be accused of being parents who were disinterested in their son's religious education. Notice this: they did not *send* Him to the temple; they *took* Him to the temple. How often modern parents send their children rather than take them to Sunday school or confirmation classes! These parents never seem to notice that in the passing of years, their divided example sets up serious barriers to their children's Christianity.

Mary and Joseph lost Jesus in the crowd. He had been gone a whole day before they missed Him. Are we to assume from this that they were bad parents who never paid much attention to the whereabouts of their pre-teen? I think not. Mary and Joseph wanted Jesus to have freedom to explore His Jewish faith. They lost Him because they refused to bear down on Him, to keep Him tightly tied to their apron strings.

Mary and Joseph did take Jesus to the temple. Within this warm and caring community of instruction (the whole thing might have taken place at Jesus' Bar Mitzvah), they gave Jesus the freedom to grow and to begin the process of separation that young people need if they are to become responsible adults. To raise responsible children, parents have to run the risk of losing them here and there along the path to maturity. But the gain is worth the risk!

Are you willing to take your own children to church even as you grant them a little freedom? Are you holding them in and letting them out in that impossible-to-do-just-right ritual of bringing up children? It's the hardest work in the world, but should your children turn out anything like Jesus, you will see how right Mary and Joseph were.

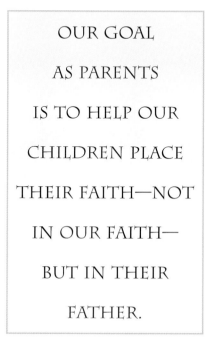

OUR GOAL

AS PARENTS

IS TO HELP OUR

CHILDREN PLACE

THEIR FAITH—NOT

IN OUR FAITH—

BUT IN THEIR

FATHER.

# AN ADDITIONAL READING

*Read: Third John 2-4*

It's scary—impossible, really—to always know exactly what to say, exactly how to set our priorities so that our children can't miss the fact that faith is real. We must always rely on God to do His own maturing work in their souls—in His time, in His way.

## PRAYER

*Lord,* thank You for great parents. Thank You for the example of strong discipline and training and the importance of church attendance. Thank You for that hard-to-develop tension between freedom and discipline. Bless my children. May I hold them in and let them go at the same time, learning from You the best time to hold on and the right time to let go.

# DECEMBER 28

*When they did not find Him, they returned to Jerusalem to search for Him. After three days, they found Him in the temple complex sitting among the teachers, listening to them and asking them questions. And all those who heard Him were astounded at His understanding and His answers.*

LUKE 2:45-47

# OF LOVE AND LEARNING

Christmas gives us a double gift—Jesus and theology. How oddly separate seem these words. Jesus and theology —can the two ever be friends?

Here in the temple they were. Many who love Jesus don't really trust theologians. How often do we meet those scholars who love theology but never seem to have much time for Jesus? They love to hide themselves in dimly lit cells with tall stacks of thick books. There they learn all they can, write all they can, and read all they can. They know all about God as a theme of study outside of themselves. They dedicate their lives to figuring out as much about God as they can in order to tell the non-scholars what they've found out.

Across the kingdom from theologians are those who love Jesus more than they study Him. They find theology boring— just plain dull and unmoving. These Jesus lovers like to *feel* their religion! They like to see people saved (which they say most theologians no longer care about) and to see people healed (theologians just go to medical specialists, they say).

The Jesus lovers read in the newspapers about theological conventions where some poorly informed scholar is always publicly doubting the virgin birth. This causes them to rail against the seminaries where scholars (or so it seems to most of the Jesus lovers) outnumber the true believers.

So it would seem that theologians and Jesus lovers are in two separate camps. *How we must avoid this error!* The scholars give us Bible translations, commentaries, and other helpful tools of study. Scholars discover manuscripts and promote archaeology, which helps us to understand the Scriptures.

Theologians, like those who distrust them, are Jesus lovers. When the two ways grow apart, faith collapses.

So do not think it odd that Jesus was in the temple with the theologians. Every Jesus lover must spend time in pursuing theology, in doing sound thinking about God. James Moffatt translated Second Timothy 3:5 like this: "They know everything about religion as a form, but will have nothing to do with it as a force in their lives." Theologians must never let that happen. So it is true for the less scholarly. Our love of Christ and our study of theology must never become separate compartments in our discipleship.

TO LOVE THE LIBRARY

IS NEVER INCONSISTENT WITH

LOVING THE LORD.

## AN ADDITIONAL READING

*Read: Second Timothy 3:14-17*

We need God's Word—not just a surface scanning nor a skimming of select phrases—but a full meal of its nourishing truth. When we merely snack on slim helpings of the Scriptures, we find ourselves strangely incomplete and ill-equipped for every good work. The New Year is upon us. Let it be the year that we lose ourselves in a love affair with God and His Word.

## PRAYER

*Lord,* I'm glad You took Your incarnate and sinless person-hood right into the presence of the theologians. Theologians who will not give You the right to be the Son of God are prac-ticing bad theology. Mystics who won't allow the church to major on great doctrines are irrelevant emotionalists. I would like to be both a thinker and a worshiper. Help me never to leave my mind at home when I go to church, nor my heart at home when I attend Bible study.

# DECEMBER 29

*W*hen His parents saw Him, they were astonished, and His mother said to Him, "Son, why have You treated us like this? Your father and I have been anxiously searching for You." "Why were you searching for Me?" He asked them. "Didn't you know that I must be involved in my Father's interests?" But they did not understand what He said to them.

LUKE 2:48-50

# THE FATHER'S BUSINESS

At just 12 years of age, did Jesus understand what His Father's business was? He might not have understood it like He did when He began his public ministry 18 years later, but He *did* understand His special calling. He understood that He was no ordinary person with ordinary reasons to live.

Even at 12 years of age, Christ was struggling to understand what is often called the "messianic conscience." This means that Jesus emptied all His God prerogatives when He became a man. Christmas is the story of the involved God. When Jesus left heaven and took on humanity, He had to struggle to gain enough of the knowledge that He had left in heaven to know how to go about redeeming the world.

So He struggled to identify what it meant to be born of a virgin. He struggled to understand what it meant to be the Son of God. He struggled to understand that before He was very old He would be the once-for-all sacrifice for the human race. He knew that He would defeat death. The immensity of being the Son of God—with all that this involved—came to Him moment by moment as He walked with God.

The idea that Jesus gradually came to understand His role as Messiah may seem strange to some, but the Bible establishes a good case for Jesus' struggle to understand His messiahship. He gradually understood who He was. One of the medieval scholars wrote that when Jesus was born, He sat up in the manger and said, "Hello, Mary, I am the Son of God!" This might argue for the godhead of Jesus, but it would not present a very good case for His humanity.

Jesus—here in the temple at age 12—knew He was God's Son. Already He had begun to understand that He had to be about His Father's business. Already He knew He would never disappoint His Father by being disobedient. Whatever it cost to redeem the human race, He knew He would pay it.

THE FATHER'S

BUSINESS HAS A

WAY OF CLEARING

THE MIND OF SELF

AND AMBITION.

## AN ADDITIONAL READING

*Read: Philippians 1:20-26*

The desire to lose ourselves in serving Christ seems so against our own dreams, we might be accused—even by well-meaning Christians—of taking our faith to a ridiculous extreme. But this hunger to be fully His—this willingness to strip away our pride, our laziness, our pet peeves, and our pleasure seeking—is not a maniacal obsession with religion. It is born in a world where all success is defined as obedience.

## PRAYER

*Lord,* thank You for being committed to Your Father's business. I was part of that business. I'm forever grateful for my salvation. That was, after all, Your Father's concern.

# DECEMBER 30

*He* went down with them and came to Nazareth, and was obedient to them. His mother kept all these things in her heart.

LUKE 2:51

# THE GOOD SON

Jesus continued in subjection to His mother and father. Does this seem an odd comment in our culture where everyone talks about freedom and few would encourage our being in submission to *anyone?*

Jesus never sinned. He never broke any of the commandments, including the fifth: "Honor your father and your mother so that your days may be prolonged in the land that the LORD your God is giving you." Adolescent rebellion is almost a virtue in our day and age. How many talk-show guests start out blaming some aspect of their ruined lives on their abusive parents?

Paul the apostle does remind parents never to be abusive to their children: "Fathers, don't stir up anger in your children, but bring them up in the training and instruction of the Lord" (Ephesians 6:4). Paul understood that parents can be abusive, and the law must deal severely with those who are.

But children have one of the Ten Commandments dedicated specifically to them: to be in subjection. Again the Apostle Paul echoes the commandment: "Children, obey your parents in the Lord, because this is right. 'Honor your father and mother'—which is the first commandment with a promise— 'that it may go well with you and that you may have a long life in the land' " (Ephesians 6:1-3).

Jesus did not need to be reminded to obey His father and mother. He lived in submission to them. How far did Jesus take this submission? Most scholars believe that Joseph died when Jesus was in His teens (Joseph is never mentioned as being alive during the years of Jesus' active ministry). Jesus, however, probably remained home until He was 30, apparently continuing to honor His dead father by serving as the family breadwinner. Jesus then continued to help support His mother until the younger children were old enough to take care of her.

Jesus believed it was a sin not to honor father and mother. Thus, He cared for Mary until it was time for His public ministry to begin. Jesus serves as a role model for all of us. We are never at liberty to dishonor our parents. Jesus taught us good family relationships by His example. Let us honor our parents as He did.

HONORING OUR PARENTS MAKES US SOMETHING LIKE THAT HOLY CHILD WHO WAS RAISED IN NAZARETH TO RULE A UNIVERSE.

## AN ADDITIONAL READING

*Read: Mark 7:9-13*

How does honoring our parents change as we move out from under their roof? It may show itself in special kindnesses— little notes that remind them how often they are in our thoughts and prayers. It may show itself in patient visits— sacrificial moments when yesterday's memories have room to minister again to them. Honor is not merely the gift of childhood but the gift of a lifetime.

## PRAYER

*Lord,* Jesus dignified all family relationships by calling You "Father." If God is my Father and I honor Him, perhaps I should let Jesus be my teacher in honoring the relationships within my family.

# DECEMBER 31

*H*e went and settled in a town called Nazareth to fulfill what was spoken through the prophets, that He will be called a Nazarene.

MATTHEW 2:23

# FROM HERE TO THERE

Jesus of Nazareth! He was indeed called "the Nazarene." To His name would forever be tied the town that was the place of His childhood and young adulthood. To this small town the entire world owes a debt. So let us exhort the great cities of our day to bow their urban heads before His humble Nazareth.

London, you are in debt to Nazareth. Tokyo, you are also. Yes, New York, you too are in debt to the little town of Nazareth.

Why? Jesus, the Son of God, made this place His training school of redemption. There in Nazareth, He studied you—you citizens of Rome, Paris, and the world. What Jesus discovered in Nazareth is that modern sophisticates are more like their ancient Nazarene counterparts than they know.

• In Nazareth or New York this New Year's Eve, people are searching for meaning.

• In Nazareth or Newfoundland, many are experiencing despair and the absence of hope.

• In Nazareth or the Netherlands, the world is hungry for self-fulfillment and the knowledge of why they came into the world.

So in Nazareth, the word *Nazarene* came to stand for more than local citizenship. Jesus the Nazarene knew Christianity would be for all people. He knew that there were no Jews or Gentiles outside the eternal circle of God's love. He knew that no one was beyond the boundaries of the worldwide community of God.

Nazareth was God's little school for the whole world. It was God's dusty little bivouac for all of human salvation. From Nazareth, it was only a little step into the hearts of all men and women.

From Nazareth, Jesus could see all the way to heaven and hell. From Nazareth, it would be easy to cry to all the world, "Come to Me, all you who are weary and burdened, and I will give you rest" (Matthew 11:28).

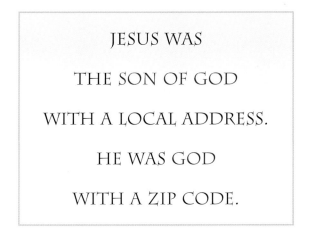

JESUS WAS

THE SON OF GOD

WITH A LOCAL ADDRESS.

HE WAS GOD

WITH A ZIP CODE.

## AN ADDITIONAL READING

*Read: Jude 24-25*

As the year draws to a close, wouldn't this be a marvelous time to begin a new chapter of faith? Wouldn't this be a momentous day to say goodbye forever to the habits that have held you below your potential? Wouldn't this be a perfect season not just to turn over a new leaf but to turn over a whole new intention? Christmas is gone, but life goes on—and on, and on, and on—for those who never stop needing the Son in their lives.

## PRAYER

*Lord,* You are the Nazarene. I am not disturbed by my differences from the Nazarenes but amazed at my similarities to them. Like them, my sin is a continual problem. Like them, I want my life to count, and I know it cannot without the presence of the great Nazarene in my life. May you ever be the One who draws my attention, who has access to my life, who can make me whatever You want me to be.

# ART ACKNOWLEDGMENTS

# ENJOY THESE OTHER BOOKS BY CALVIN MILLER

*Continue your devotional reading into the new year with these rich, expressive books on the life of Christ.*

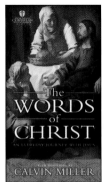

*The Words of Christ*
1-5864-0010-X

*Until He Comes*
0-8054-1654-4

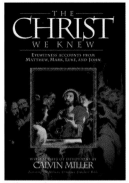

*The Christ We Knew*
0-8054-9415-4